Delegating
Work

Pocket Mentor Series

The *Pocket Mentor* Series offers immediate solutions to common challenges managers face on the job every day. Each book in the series is packed with handy tools, self-tests, and real-life examples to help you identify your strengths and weaknesses and hone critical skills. Whether you're at your desk, in a meeting, or on the road, these portable guides enable you to tackle the daily demands of your work with greater speed, savvy, and effectiveness.

Delegating Work

Expert Solutions to Everyday Challenges

Harvard Business Press

Boston, Massachusetts

Copyright 2008 Harvard Business School Publishing Corporation

Printed in the United States of America

12 11 10 09 08   5 4 3 2 1

Library of Congress Cataloging-in-Publication Data

Delegating work : expert solutions to everyday challenges.

    p. cm. — (Pocket mentor series)

  Includes bibliographical references.

  ISBN 978-1-4221-1877-1

  1. Delegation of authority. 2. Supervision of employees. I. Harvard Business School Publishing Corporation.

  HD50.D45 2008

  658.3'128—dc22

                                                                    2007037465

The paper used in this publication meets the requirements of the American National Standard for Permanence of Paper for Publications and Documents in Libraries and Archives Z39.48-1992.

Contents

Tips and Tools 55

Tools for Delegating 57

Worksheets to help you assess your delegating skills, prepare to delegate, track a delegated assignment, and select personnel for a delegated task.

Test Yourself 63

A helpful review of concepts presented in this guide. To see how much you've learned, take it before and after you've read the guide.

Answers to test questions 66

Frequently Asked Questions 69

Answers to common queries regarding delegating.

To Learn More 71

Titles of articles and books if you want to go more deeply into the topic.

Sources for Delegating Work 77

Notes 79

For you to use as ideas come to mind.

Mentor's Message: Why Master the Art of Delegation?

Is your in-box always full? Do you regularly work overtime on tasks that "only you" can do? If you answered yes to either of these questions, then you probably could benefit from delegating some of your workload.

Delegating offers many advantages to you, your direct reports, and your company. For you, delegating gives you more time to focus on projects that require your particular skills and authority. For your *direct reports*, delegating can increase motivation by helping individuals enhance existing skills and develop new ones—and can also strengthen trust and communication between you and your group. For your *company*, effective delegation ensures that the right person, at the right level, performs a task, thereby improving overall efficiency and productivity.

Despite these benefits, many managers feel uneasy about delegating. Why? Some fear losing control of staff and projects and worry that they're abdicating responsibility. Others, pressed for time, simply do the job themselves rather than make time in their schedules to teach someone else. Still others shy away from delegating because they've had a bad experience—for example, a delegated assignment was poorly done or a deadline was missed.

In the long term, however, such fears are rarely justified if you delegate effectively. This guide helps you reap the many benefits of delegating. It shows you how to select a delegation approach, lay the groundwork for a successful delegation, make delegated assignments, and monitor work that you've delegated.

Although learning to delegate may take practice, the rewards are well worth the time and energy you put into mastering this key business skill.

Thomas L. Brown, Mentor

Thomas L. Brown is the author of more than four hundred published articles on managerial leadership. He wrote the first online book on leadership, *The Anatomy Of Fire: Sparking A New Spirit Of Enterprise*, which explores the look and feel of leadership in the twenty-first century. Tom has written for many publications, including *IndustryWeek*, *Harvard Management Update*, *Financial Times*, and the *Wall Street Journal*, and has presented to dozens of major corporations.

Delegating Work: The Basics

What Is
Delegating?

To MASTER THE BASICS of delegating, let's start by exploring its purpose and benefits as well as common concerns that managers have about the subject. The following sections address each of these in detail. An additional section helps you determine whether your delegating skills need improvement.

The purpose of delegating

Put most simply, delegation involves the assignment of a specific task or project by one person to another, and the assignee's commitment to complete it. When you delegate, you not only transfer responsibility to another person but also transfer accountability for maintaining established standards. Delegating is one of the most important skills demonstrated by successful managers and one often neglected or overlooked by overworked managers. You know you're delegating effectively if you're spending less time "doing" and more time planning work assignments, organizing resources, and coaching people who need help.

The benefits of delegating

Effective delegation can have important benefits for you, your people, and your organization. Let's start with you. When you delegate, you can reduce your workload and stress level by removing from your to-do list tasks that others are qualified to do. This increases the time you have to focus on projects that require your particular skills and authority. It also enables you to take on higher-level efforts such as planning, conducting business analyses, controlling operations, obtaining resources, and dealing with key people problems.

Delegating also improves the level of trust between you and your staff. To get trust, you must first give trust, and delegating is one way to do it. The message in delegation is, "I trust you to get the job done." It also helps everyone learn how to achieve goals through cooperative effort.

Delegating also is an effective way of testing a staff member's capabilities before you offer a promotion. If you assign a series of tasks to an employee, you'll soon have a good estimate of that person's strengths and weaknesses.

Good employees benefit from the delegation of tasks and projects. Every assignment is an opportunity to learn how to accept responsibility, to plan work, and to enlist the cooperation of others. In effect, delegating gives employees experience with managerial work. And developing people is part of your job.

The table "The benefits of delegating" sums up the key advantages that delegating offers to you, your staff, and your organization.

Common managerial concerns about delegating

Delegation makes some managers uneasy. They fear losing control of staff and projects, and they worry that they're abdicating responsibility. Sometimes they just believe that doing the job themselves

What Would YOU Do?

The Case of the Harried Handoff

TRAVIS HAS JUST received an e-mail saying that his group has won the key Jardin Estates development deal. Travis cannot think of anyone in his group who has time to run the project, and he certainly does not have time to handle it himself. After a brief meeting about the group's workload, Jill pops into Travis's office, smiling and volunteering to take charge. Travis is skeptical. Jill is bright and enthusiastic, but she has only two years of experience. Travis does not want to see Jill—or his group—fail, especially with this important client. Should he risk handing the job over to Jill? Or is there some other solution?

What would YOU do? The mentor will suggest a solution in *What You COULD Do.*

---

will be most efficient. In the long term, however, these fears and beliefs are rarely justified. The table "Common arguments against delegating" shows common arguments against delegating and counters them with reasoned responses and ideas.

In addition to harboring concerns about delegating, many managers struggle with four problems in trying to delegate. First, it's difficult to watch someone else grapple with a task that you know you could do easily in half the time. Practice keeping silent;

The benefits of delegating

Who gains benefits	How delegating benefits
You	• Improves the level of trust and communication between you and your staff • Achieves goals that require cooperative group effort
Your staff	• Improves the level of trust and communication between you and your staff • Achieves goals that require cooperative group effort
Your organization	• Saves money by ensuring that tasks are assigned to the right person at the right level • Increases overall productivity and efficiency by making the best use of organizational resources

interceding will only frustrate your subordinate, not to mention using the time you wanted to save!

> **Tip:** Let go of your need to have a say in how tasks are accomplished. Consider delegation as a way to develop the skills of your staff or to position people favorably with senior management. And trust your staff's ability to get the job done.

Second, delegating can trigger a kind of identity crisis for managers. It means shifting from the role of specialist—whether in finance, marketing, or some other function—to that of generalist. It

Common arguments against delegating

Argument	Response
"I can do this better and quicker than my staff."	Perhaps you can, but the goal is to support your staff in doing the work.
"I don't have confidence in my staff."	Start by delegating small tasks and projects that will allow you to build confidence gradually.
"It's easier to do it myself than to organize it, explain it, and monitor it."	This is a short-term view. In general, the time spent planning the project will be worth it, and, over time, your employees will be able to take on more responsibility for structuring and planning their own assignments.
"I like to have things done my way."	Focus your energies on communicating your preferences and quality standards rather than on controlling the tasks themselves. This investment will pay off not only for the current project, but also for future projects.
"My staff will resent the additional work" or "My staff expect me to be the problem solver and decision maker."	Manage the expectations. Make it clear that your role is to support your staff in making decisions for themselves. Also, make it clear that this means they will get opportunities to do new and interesting work. Make sure you follow through.

means becoming a leader, and leaders don't have such precise job definitions. To delegate, you must give up the particular skills for which you've become known—and the gratification that goes with applying them.

Third, you may experience a feeling of competitiveness as you watch while others, thriving on the challenges associated with handling delegated assignments, reach ability levels superior to your own. Delegating means letting others become the experts.

Fourth, becoming an effective delegator means learning a whole new job. Instead of handling day-to-day details and other people's problems, you focus on where your unit should be heading in terms of strategic direction. You must secure agreement on that direction from your subordinates and keep your unit on track. Learning this new job may mean leaving your comfort zone. It means learning the art of leadership.

These are difficult challenges, especially for novice managers. But the following practices can help you delegate effectively in spite of them:

- **Recruit the best.** The sum of your unit is really its human resources, and high-quality people are the base from which your unit can make its best contribution to the organization overall. To fulfill its function in the company, your unit needs the best possible employees—people who can take on new tasks, learn from them, strengthen their skills, and make informed decisions. For that reason, you should do what you can to attract top-quality people. You may need to get creative. For example, ask vendors and customers to recommend potential new hires. They make excellent recruiting sources, because they know the people in your business.

- **Practice "what and why" management.** Your people can't handle a delegated task effectively unless they understand in crystal-clear terms *what* is expected of them. They also need to know *why* the task is important to the unit and the organization. People are more motivated when they understand the reasons for doing things in a certain way than when they are simply given rules. We all want to believe in what we're doing, and we want to know the importance of our work. Knowing the "why" fulfills these needs.

- **Think effectively.** As you free up more of your own time through delegating, continually ask and answer the question, "What's next?" Your unit can't deliver top performance without a clear picture of where it's going. Once you've envisioned your unit's future, you can share that image with your team. It's this shared vision that generates the impetus for excellence. But thinking effectively isn't about attending meetings, writing reports, or handling other day-to-day matters. Instead, it's about reflecting on what's going on in your company and industry, coming up with ideas you haven't previously considered, and getting excited about the possibilities of the future. To that end, ensure that you get enough time to think, even if it means scheduling large blocks of uninterrupted time during periods when you're at your best. For example, if the beginning of the week is your "prime time," schedule Monday mornings as your thinking time. Then make the most of your thinking time by recording, sorting, and saving your thoughts. Files containing ideas about your unit's and company's future are your most important store of information.

Delegating versus empowerment

The term *empowerment* has been bandied about over the past five or ten years. Is this term synonymous with delegation? If not, how is it different?

Delegation implies that the manager retains authority, control, and responsibility. To do otherwise would be abdication. The manager says, "This is what I'd like you to do." Even if she describes the required ends without specifying the means, she will probably review the employee's plan and monitor his performance as it unfolds. In the absence of authority, control, and responsibility, delegation is abandonment.

Empowerment, on the other hand, shifts power and responsibility to the recipient. The empowered individual or team has the authority to determine the means and takes responsibility for results. Self-discipline and accountability are substitutes for the manager's control.

Do your delegating skills need improvement?

Let's look at some common warning signs that you may need to learn how to delegate more effectively.

- Your in-box is always full. You are regularly working overtime on tasks that "only you" can do.
- You are frequently interrupted by requests for guidance and clarification of work assignments.
- Direct reports feel they are being "dumped on" and lack the authority to complete assignments.
- Direct reports feel inadequately prepared to carry out assigned tasks.
- You frequently intervene in tasks or projects assigned to one of your staff.

- You second-guess staff decisions and personally redo unsatisfactory staff assignments.

- Your staff members are not taking responsibility for the tasks or projects you delegate.

- Morale is low, and staff turnover is on the rise.

- Delegated assignments are incomplete, and deadlines are being missed.

If many of the situations in this list are true for you, then there's no doubt about it: you would benefit substantially from strengthening your delegation skills.

What You COULD Do.

Remember Travis's worries about who should handle the Jardin Estates project?

Here's what the mentor suggests:

The first thing Travis should do is evaluate the work involved and determine what skills are needed. If Jill has the necessary skills, Travis might want to delegate the project to her and work closely with her to monitor progress during the project.

If Travis feels that the Jardin Estates development deal requires a more senior manager, he might consider acting as the lead on the project and delegating most of the work to the project team members. In this case, Travis, a seasoned manager, would be overseeing the key account, but he would also be giving employees an opportunity to take on new responsibilities as they gain experience.

Guidelines
for Effective
Delegating

TO LAY THE groundwork for successful delegating, you need to first establish the right environment and then select a delegation approach; that is, will you delegate by task, by project, or by function? The following sections explore each of these in more detail.

Establishing the right environment

How do you establish the right tone and environment for effective delegating? The most successful managers follow these guidelines:

- Encourage your staff to share their special interests and time availability for new projects.

- Build a sense of shared responsibility for the unit's overall goals.

- Avoid dumping only tedious or difficult jobs on your staff. Instead, delegate projects and tasks that spark staff interest and can be enjoyable.

- Provide possible career opportunities for staff members by delegating projects, tasks, or functions that involve high visibility with your manager or a high-level manager in another organization.

- Delegate to people whose judgment and competence you trust. Your ability to select the right person reflects your skill in making decisions and setting goals.

- Recognize that delegation is a learning experience for you and your staff, and offer training or coaching as needed.

- Develop trust in a less-skilled staff member by delegating highly structured assignments and providing the support needed for the person to develop increased competence.

- Whenever possible, delegate an entire project or function, and not only a small piece; this practice will likely increase motivation and commitment.

- Create clear guidelines for follow-up, monitoring, and feedback.

- Maintain open lines of communication. Say, "Let me know if you run into any problems you cannot handle."

- To minimize wasted time and resources and to ensure that the task, project, or function is completed successfully, clearly define goals, expected outcomes, and measures of success.

Selecting a delegation approach

It is usually best to delegate responsibility for an entire task, project, or function to one person rather than divide it among a number of people. This practice helps eliminate confusion and encourages initiative and problem-solving. If that person then involves others, it is clear to everyone who is ultimately responsible for the outcome.

Once you've identified a person to whom you want to delegate, consider whether you will delegate by task, project, or function:

- **Delegating by task.** Delegating by task is the easiest approach and a good place to start. It involves assigning specific tasks or subtasks to staff members. These might include writing a report, conducting research, or planning a meeting.

- **Delegating by project.** A project involves a group of tasks designed to achieve a specific objective. Delegating by project increases the scope of the delegation assignment and generally requires a staff member who can handle a wider range of responsibilities. Examples of project delegations include developing a new employee handbook, conducting a customer survey, or training employees on a new computer system.

- **Delegating by function.** Some managers with large numbers of direct reports may choose to delegate assignments by function. "Function" here refers to groups of tasks and projects that are related to one ongoing activity such as sales, marketing, or training. In this model, each function is delegated to one staff member, who provides the manager with regular updates on activities within that function.

Preparing to
Delegate

A S YOU PREPARE to delegate, you first need to clarify in your own mind the purpose of the delegation. You also need to decide what to delegate—and what not to delegate—as well as identify the skills required for the assignment and match the right person to the task. Following are guidelines for tackling each of these challenges.

Identifying your reasons for delegating

What is your purpose for delegating a particular assignment? Do you want to decrease your workload? Encourage staff members to develop new skills? Launch an entirely new project or function? Provide staff members with visibility and recognition?

By identifying your reasons for delegating, you can more easily assess how well you've achieved your purpose once the assignment has been carried out.

Deciding what to delegate

Assess your own workload to determine which tasks, projects, or functions to consider for delegation. Some jobs can be performed readily by others but are jobs you have always done or enjoy doing and don't want to give up. They may include carrying out complicated production tasks, fielding requests for information or materials, analyzing your budget, or managing a staff member. Be open to delegating these tasks. Some of them can add variety to staff workload and provide motivational challenge to the right individuals.

Other jobs could be performed by others who have the right training or experience. Delegating these assignments can give staff members opportunities to develop new skills and talents and can increase the pool of people who can take responsibility for critical assignments.

If a task is too important to delegate to someone else, think about sharing responsibility. For instance, think of ways to subdivide a task so that you handle a discrete part of the task and delegate the rest.

EXAMPLE: Clara decided to share responsibility for the important task of evaluating potential new database software for her department. She handled one part of this task: reviewing the proposals from software companies. She delegated other parts of the task, such as contacting the potential companies and compiling the proposals.

But times had changed. Now that he was the department manager, Colin had little time to spare. He could still do this job himself, but that would involve many weekends in the office and would take time from other pressing responsibilities.

In the end, Colin formed a task force. He provided leadership and oversight, and two new employees with good analytical skills

What Would YOU Do?

A Vision of a Venue

PAULA RUNS A department in Vision-Able, a large management consultancy that produces annual conferences featuring big-name executives from the corporate world. A resort that usually hosts the conferences that take place on the West Coast is shutting down. Paula knows that her department will need to research other venue options for the West Coast conferences, and she'd like to delegate the project to one of her team members.

Anil strikes her as a possible good match for the project. He has the thinking skills—particularly logical thinking—needed for the job. He knows how to carry out the activities required by the project, such as comparing the amenities offered by various venues and analyzing the costs. And he has the needed interpersonal skills, including the ability to negotiate effectively with vendors. In fact, the more Paula considers Anil as a possible choice for delegating the project, the better she feels about him.

Still, she wants to be sure she's selecting the right person for the job. She wonders whether there are other considerations she should take into account in addition to analyzing the work involved and the skills required. Yet she's not sure what other questions she should ask herself.

What would YOU do? The mentor will suggest a solution in *What You COULD Do.*

were assigned the time-consuming parts of the job. When the final survey report was circulated within the company, it bore the names of Colin and his two helpers.

EXAMPLE: One of Colin's responsibilities during the first half of this year was to design, administer, and document an annual employee survey. This was a big job, but not so big that Colin couldn't handle it himself, as he had in previous years.

But times had changed. Now that he was the department manager, Colin had little time to spare. He could still do this job himself, but that would involve many weekends in the office and would take time from other pressing responsibilities.

In the end, Colin formed a task force. He provided leadership and oversight, and two new employees with good analytical skills were assigned the time-consuming parts of the job. When the final survey report was circulated within the company, it bore the names of Colin and his two helpers.

Knowing what not to delegate

Not all tasks, projects, and functions should be delegated. As a manager, you should retain responsibility for tasks such as these:

- Planning, directing, and motivating your team
- Evaluating employee performance
- Handling complex customer negotiations
- Performing tasks requiring your specific set of technical skills
- Hiring and firing staff members and helping your direct reports develop their careers

Also, consider the commonly asked question, "How can I avoid having staff members feel that I'm dumping work on them?" Some managers make the mistake of pushing every chore onto the one or two employees who (a) have demonstrated that they can get things done or (b) accept added work—unlike others—without having a tantrum. These reliable individuals may be flattered by their boss's confidence in them, at least for a while. But too much of this can create a backlash, especially when those who take on the added work don't feel that they are being compensated for it. "Why does she always ask me to handle these chores?" they may be muttering. "I'm not the only person in this department." Resentment can lead to malingering or even defection.

Tip: To decide what to delegate, identify routine tasks, specific projects, or complete functions that could easily be done by other staff members or outside resources; those that could be done by others with a minimum of coaching or on-the-job training; and those that could be completed by a staff member if additional training or coaching were provided by you or a staff peer.

You can avoid this problem by balancing the assignment of tasks seen as tedious or difficult with tasks and projects that spark staff interest, can be enjoyable, and may gain them recognition by others. To promote a sense of shared responsibility for jobs seen as boring or unpleasant, split these tasks or projects among more than one staff member and do a few yourself. And seek input from your staff about the types of assignments they find interesting and challenging.

Identifying skills required for the assignment

You cannot select the best person for a given assignment until you have analyzed the work and determined the skills that are required. The analysis involves answering these three questions:

- What kinds of **thinking skills** are needed for this job? (For example, does the work require problem-solving ability, logical thinking, decision making, planning, or creative design?)

- What are the **activities** that must be performed, and what **systems or equipment** will be needed? (Do the activities include creating a new database, organizing, training, or developing?)

- What **interpersonal skills** are needed to complete the assignment? (Will the assignee need to speak with suppliers, negotiate for resources, or consult with experts?)

Matching the right person to the task

Ask yourself, "Which of my direct reports is the right person for the job?" Compare the skills required with the characteristics and capabilities of each of your staff members. Be sure to consider these factors:

- Any previously expressed needs or desires for growth and development that could be addressed with this assignment. Ask yourself who has shown initiative and asked for a new challenge.

- Each staff member's availability. You may want to avoid choosing an employee whose work on another project would be interrupted.

- The number of previous assignments you have delegated to that person. Try to delegate tasks among all staff members to avoid feelings of favoritism.

- The level of assistance a staff member would need from you to complete the assignment and how much time you have available.

- How long the staff member has been on the job. Avoid overloading new employees with added assignments until they are comfortable with their new jobs.

- The possibility of dividing the task between two or more people to make the best use of skills.

If you routinely keep track of special skills that you may need to call upon for special projects, you'll be in a better position to select the right people. For example, someone who can simplify abstract concepts might be a good trainer, and good organizational abilities would be important for someone overseeing operations.

Tip: To make the best use of staff resources, always delegate to the lowest possible skill level required.

Steps for Delegating to the Right Person

1. **Be aware of the skills associated with specific tasks or functions.**
   Certain kinds of conceptual abilities are often associated with specific tasks or functions. As you delegate, it is important to keep these kinds of skills in mind to ensure that you make the most effective match of tasks and people.

2. **Become familiar with your own strengths and weaknesses and those of your staff.**
   Be clear about what each member of your staff can and cannot do. Don't assume that skills are transferable to all situations. For instance, a great telephone sales representative may freeze in a face-to-face selling situation.

   - Don't be afraid to take advantage of the skills of more than one person in completing a task. For instance, one person with excellent writing skills might write the text for a new brochure and then pass it on to another person with graphics and production skills to complete layout and final development.
   - Challenge your staff members with assignments that test their skills so that they can discover new capabilities.
   - Keep track of special skills that you may need to call upon for special projects.

3. **Coordinate everyone's skills to achieve the most complementary fit.**
   When you have a pool of skills to choose from, pairing up people with complementary skills can help you achieve the best results. To

illustrate, you might ask one staff member with great people skills to conduct telephone interviews with customers, and a second person with great analytical skills to examine the feedback and write a report. Knowing your staff's strengths and weaknesses can help you assemble the best team for any assignment.

4. **If necessary, look for resources outside your own group, and don't forget your supervisor as a possible resource.**
   At times you cannot find the skills you need for a specific assignment within your staff or you have exhausted the use of your own resources. Look outside your own group to colleagues or other departments for the expertise you need, and offer to exchange services in return for their assistance. Don't be reluctant to delegate to your supervisor if that seems appropriate.

5. **Consider using resources outside your organization.**
   At times you need to consider the use of outside consultants or temporary workers to

   - Fill short-term gaps in staffing
   - Provide specific expertise
   - Conduct an independent evaluation
   - Help in long-term planning
   - Save time and money over the long term

Before hiring any consultant, check references and obtain a written proposal that addresses your needs. Be aware that you will need to manage any consultants or temporary workers.

What You COULD Do.

Remember Paula's concern about whether Anil would make the best match for the venue-research project?

Here's what the mentor suggests:

Paula has taken a good first step in analyzing the work involved and the skills required and in assessing how well Anil might fit the bill. In addition, Paula should take other matters into account, such as Anil's availability, his desire to take on a developmental opportunity, and the amount of help she would need to provide in order for him to successfully handle the assignment. If she still feels that Anil has the skills for and interest in the project but that his plate is already full, she might consider reassigning some of his work to another team member to free up Anil's time. Or she could give Anil primary responsibility for the project and suggest that he get additional help from one or two other staff members.

Making the Assignment

WHENEVER YOU DELEGATE an assignment, you discuss the work with the assignee you've selected and you determine the degree of authority over the work that you will grant to the assignee. Following are suggestions for handling each of these matters.

Setting up the discussion

Once you've identified the right person for the task, you need to communicate the proposition clearly. Ideally, you should do this in a face-to-face meeting in which you describe the assignment and secure the employee's commitment to perform the task. Open communication and trust are critical factors in this interaction. To achieve both, make sure to cover the following in your discussion:

- Clearly describe the task, project, or function.

- Define its purpose and explain how it fits into the big picture.

- Review the scope of the employee's responsibilities.

- Identify other personnel who will be involved, if applicable, and describe their roles.

- Discuss feasible deadlines for completion.

- Establish agreed-upon standards of performance, measures of success, and levels of accountability.

- Set firm metrics for such things as quality, time, and cost.

- Be clear about the employee's accountability in meeting the standards you have agreed upon.

- Define the resources and support that will be available.

- Identify any materials and physical resources needed to complete the assignment, and confirm their availability.

- If necessary, allocate additional staff to assist in meeting the assigned goals.

- Ask the employee what support she thinks she may need from you throughout the assignment.

- If special training or coaching is needed, discuss how it will be given.

- Agree on a date to review progress.

Tip: Explain assignments clearly, and provide resources needed for successful completion.

Steps for Communicating a Delegated Assignment

1. **Set up a face-to-face meeting with the person to whom you are delegating an assignment.**

   - A critical component of the delegation process is the interaction between you and your employee at the time the delegation is made. This should be done in person.

   - It is always a good idea to follow up this meeting with a written memo outlining the key points of the discussion. You can do this yourself or request that your staff member do it.

2. **Clearly describe the task, project, or function.**

   - Define the purpose of the assignment, and explain how it fits into the big picture.

   - Review the scope of the employee's responsibilities.

   - Identify other personnel who will be involved, if applicable, and describe their roles.

   - Discuss feasible deadlines for completion.

   - Pass along any information the assignee needs to get started.

3. **Establish agreed-upon standards of performance, measures of success, and levels of accountability.**

   - Set firm benchmarks for such things as quality, time, and cost.

   - Be clear with the employee about his accountability in meeting the standards you have agreed upon.

4. **Define the resources and support that will be available.**

- Identify any materials and physical resources needed to complete the assignment, and confirm their availability.

- If necessary, allocate additional staff to assist in meeting the assigned goals.

- Ask the employee what support he thinks he may need from you throughout the assignment.

5. **Identify the need for any special training or coaching, and describe how it will be given.**

- If the assignment requires the staff member to develop new skills, agree upon an appropriate plan for training.

- Discuss the need for coaching, and set up a schedule agreeable to both parties to provide the needed support.

- Agree upon a date to review progress, and assess the need for additional training or continued coaching.

6. **Clearly define the level of authority being delegated.**
   Be sure to clearly define the level of authority you are delegating, and ensure that it meets the needs of the assignment. Depending on the employee's capabilities and your confidence in him, you may choose to allow him to do one of the following:

- Make and implement decisions as needed without prior consultation with you.

- Make decisions as needed and notify you before any implementation.

- Make recommendations for a final decision, which you must then approve.

- Provide you with several alternatives from which you will make a final decision.

- Provide you with relevant information from which you will develop alternatives and then make a decision with input from the staff member.

Take the initiative in communicating the authority you have delegated to other involved staff members. In determining the level of authority to delegate, consider your confidence in the staff member's abilities and the complexity of the task or project involved.

7. **Agree upon parameters for follow-up and feedback.**

- Establish a system for reporting progress regularly—for example, monthly reports, or weekly or monthly staff meetings.

- Agree upon parameters for providing ongoing feedback as needed. Your feedback will be seen as less intrusive if you and your staff member agree ahead of time about when and how you will provide it.

- Establish how and when you will become involved if the expected goals of the task, project, or function are at risk or if other major problems arise.

Granting authority

In granting authority to a staff member, you must establish clear guidelines and expectations from the start. The amount of authority you choose to give an individual depends upon his capabilities and your confidence in him. You will want to do the following:

- Assess the staff member's past performance in making decisions.

- Consider the consequences of wrong decisions and decide what degree of risk you are willing to take.

- Determine the minimum amount of authority needed to complete the assignment successfully.

Based on your insights into these matters, determine the range of authority levels you want to delegate.

After you have determined the level of authority you will delegate, be sure to communicate your decision to everyone involved in the assignment.

Monitoring a Delegation

DELEGATING DOESN'T end with assigning a task, project, or function to a member of your staff. You also need to monitor the delegation to ensure that everything goes as planned. Keys to monitoring include tracking the delegated assignment, providing support, handling "reverse delegation," addressing problems, and reflecting on the experience so that you can apply learning to your next delegation.

The following sections examine each of these in turn.

Tracking a delegated assignment

One of the greatest challenges for the delegating manager is to ensure that the employee does not fail. The best way to ensure success is to maintain an adequate level of control by providing target completion dates and regular monitoring of progress. When you say, "I want this done by next Friday," you are maintaining control of the work, as is your duty as manager. When you add, "I'd like to meet with you on Wednesday afternoon, just to see how you're progressing and to discuss any problems," you are monitoring the delegated assignment. Monitoring provides opportunities to give coaching and feedback, another key responsibility of every manager.

Depending on the number and complexity of delegated assignments, you can use one or more of the following techniques for monitoring:

- Referral folders for each task or project

- An assignment log that tracks all projects, tasks, or functions in your department

- A giant wall calendar

- Staff meetings

- Written status reports

- Project management and tracking software

In monitoring, be alert to early signs of trouble. When your subordinate hits an impenetrable barrier or begins to fall behind, it may be necessary to intervene. Of course, you don't want to solve every problem that you've delegated to others and that they have accepted. Doing so would defeat your purpose. So use coaching, encouragement, and added resources as you see fit to help them help themselves. Provide this support without being intrusive, especially for subordinates who are committed to learning how to handle things by themselves, and without dictating the "right way." Remember that accomplishing the task is more important than your idea of *how* it should be accomplished.

What Would YOU Do?

No Visible Signs of Support

THE BIGGEST THING on Martin's plate is an upcoming product launch—a time-consuming effort that he hasn't even started. Members of his group have expressed an interest in taking on more responsibility, and each has different strengths. Martin decides to delegate the product launch to a staff member. He identifies the particular skills required to handle the assignment and decides that Joy is the best match. She knows the product well and has worked on product launches before, although she hasn't led one. Joy likes independence and works well on her own—and she is eager to prove herself.

A few weeks have passed since Martin delegated the product launch to Joy. Planning has steadily progressed. Joy is excited to have the added responsibility and feels confident that all is going well. Martin is pleased with her performance—and pleased that he has more time for other work.

But one day, during a routine meeting with the marketing group, Martin finds out that the group is unusually busy. He knows that marketing plays an essential role in a successful product launch, and he is concerned that it may not complete the marketing materials in time for the launch. He's unsure about what to do. Should he mention his concerns directly to the marketing group, or will that make Joy feel that he is taking back responsibility for the product launch? Should he assume that Joy will know how to deal with the marketing deadlines? How can he best support her while ensuring that the product launch is carried out successfully?

What would YOU do? The mentor will suggest a solution in *What You COULD Do.*

Providing support

Once you have delegated an assignment, you need to continue to provide support without being intrusive. You strike the right balance when you do these things:

- Notify all relevant personnel of the authority you have delegated with the assignment.

- Review resource needs and ensure that appropriate supplies are available.

- Continue to supply any needed information, such as reference materials or reports, that may have a bearing on the assignment.

- Make clear when you want to be involved; for example, you need to be involved when it looks as if a commitment won't be met or when major problems have arisen.

- After work begins, intercede with advice or directions only if requested.

- Point out any difficulties you may see ahead based on your experience with similar projects.

- Remember to focus on results and not on the methods or approach used to achieve them.

Tip: Provide ongoing feedback to your assignees, and support them through their mistakes.

Handling reverse delegation

Reverse delegation occurs when a staff member to whom you have delegated an assignment either wants to return the job to you or expects you to solve problems and make decisions. Resist the temptation to step in. This is an opportunity for you to build trust and confidence in your employee by doing the following:

- Providing positive reinforcement for the work done so far

- Helping the employee assess the situation

- Confirming your confidence in the employee's ability to make decisions

- Encouraging the employee to come up with a solution

- Providing coaching as needed to help the employee refine her new skills

For a deeper understanding of the damage that reverse delegation can cause, imagine this scenario. You're racing down the hall. An employee stops you and says, "We've got a problem on that project you assigned me." You assume you should get involved, but you don't have time to make an on-the-spot decision. You say, "Let me think about it."

You've just allowed what some managers call a "monkey" to leap from your subordinate's back to yours. You're now working for your subordinate. When you take on a lot of monkeys by accepting reverse delegation, you don't have time to handle your real job: fulfilling your own boss's mandates and helping peers generate business results.

To avoid accumulating monkeys, you need to develop your subordinates' initiative. For example, when an employee tries to hand you a problem, clarify whether he should recommend and implement a solution, take action, and then brief you immediately, or act and report the outcome at a regular update.

When you encourage employees to handle their own monkeys, they acquire new skills—and you liberate time to do your own job.

The following suggestions can help you return monkeys to their rightful owners:

- **Make appointments to deal with monkeys.** Avoid discussing any monkey on an ad hoc basis—for example, when you pass a subordinate in the hallway. You won't convey the proper seriousness. Instead, schedule an appointment to discuss the issue.

- **Specify the level of initiative you want from your employee.** Your employees can exercise five levels of initiative in handling on-the-job problems. From lowest to highest, here are the levels:

  1. Wait until told what to do.

  2. Ask what to do.

  3. Recommend an action, and then, with your approval, implement it.

  4. Take independent action but advise you at once.

  5. Take independent action and update you through routine procedures.

  When an employee brings a problem to you, outlaw the use of level 1 or 2. Agree on and assign level 3, 4, or 5 to the monkey. Take no more than fifteen minutes to discuss the problem.

- **Agree on a status update.** After deciding how to proceed, agree on a time and place when the employee will give you a progress report.

- **Examine your own motives.** As we've seen, some managers secretly worry that if they encourage subordinates to take more initiative, they'll appear less strong, more vulnerable, and less useful. Instead of harboring these worries, cultivate an inward sense of security that frees you to relinquish direct control and support employees' growth.

- **Develop your employees' skills.** Employees try to hand off monkeys when they lack the desire or ability to handle them. Help employees develop needed problem-solving skills. It's initially more time-consuming than tackling problems yourself, but it saves time in the long run.

- **Foster trust.** Developing employees' initiative requires a trusting relationship between you and your subordinates. If they're afraid of failing, they'll keep bringing their monkeys to you rather than work to solve their own problems. To promote trust, reassure them it's safe to make mistakes.

Addressing problems

There may be situations when you need to reassess a staff member's ability to complete an assignment successfully. In most cases, your employee will be able to work through his difficulties with your assistance. You can help get the project back on track by doing the following:

- Completing selected parts of the assignment to lighten the load on the employee

- Offering additional resources, if available, to provide assistance

- Helping the employee solve problems without placing blame for any difficulties

- Treating mistakes as growth opportunities rather than punishable offenses

- Creating an agreed-upon plan of action and a timetable for addressing the problems

Only in extreme cases should you consider taking back the delegation. Do this only if major problems are evident: if critical deadlines will be missed or if failure to meet established goals will have a serious negative impact on other projects.

Experts offer these additional suggestions for "delegating so it sticks":

- **Make yourself let go.** Effective delegation hinges on reexamining two basic assumptions about your role as a manager. First, many managers assume that it's faster and more efficient to take on employees' problems than to teach them to handle their own. Second, many assume that they know more than their direct reports do. Both assumptions can increase your desire to control problem solving and decision making rather than foster a sense of accountability and initiative in your employees. To counteract this, think of yourself as a leader, not a manager. Managers deal with details, whereas leaders encourage a sense of ownership and accountability among subordinates. By envisioning yourself as a leader, you become more comfortable and open to delegating tasks initially and to return problems to employees. Whenever you micromanage your people, you send the message that you don't need them.

- **Ask, don't tell.** Letting go of problems is only as effective as the manner in which you delegate them. To that end, when you're delegating, ask questions rather than dictate orders. When you say, "What do you think should be done to handle this project?" you teach your people to come up with ideas and possible solutions whenever they work on a delegated task or grapple with a problem at work. And open-ended questions—such as "What things might we consider if we implement the solution you're proposing?"—can reveal the degree to which your employee has thought about the problem or delegated task. In addition to questions, silences after an employee has offered an idea can help give the person ample time to evaluate the idea and possibly generate additional ones.

- **Cultivate independent thinking.** The more your employees think independently and feel a sense of ownership in their jobs, the more they'll be able to embrace delegated assignments and resolve problems themselves. To encourage independent thinking, let your direct reports know that you want them to make you aware of any problems that arise as they handle a delegated task—but that you also want them to come prepared with observations and multiple suggestions for how they'll solve the problem.

- **Make sure people have access to the resources they need.**
  Linking your direct reports with the resources they need to
  carry out a delegated task and solve problems can further
  help you delegate successfully. Think of resources in broad
  terms—people, tools, information, and development opportunities that can help employees resolve issues and handle assignments on their own. Serving as a "resource
  connector" can be as simple as saying, "You need to talk to
  Joe in marketing." Information tools can also be valuable—
  for instance, an intranet phone directory organized by
  department and function, and not by name, for new
  employees who don't yet know anyone but who need to
  know where to bring specific concerns while handling a
  delegated task.

Reflecting on a completed assignment

To process lessons learned from delegation, you need to step back
and reflect at the conclusion of each assignment. Set up an evaluation discussion with your employee. Here are guidelines for the
discussion:

- Ask for the employee's opinion about how this delegation
  worked for her.

- Recognize the employee's achievements, and provide positive reinforcement for tasks done well.

- Compare the results with the expected standards.

- Avoid criticism and blame for any problems, and discuss possible improvements for future projects.

- Create a plan of action to continue to support the employee's growth through ongoing coaching or additional training.

You should also take steps to ensure that your employee gets recognition for her work—not only from you but also from your peers, your manager, and the customer, as appropriate.

Teaching delegation skills to team leaders

Reflecting on completed assignments can be a valuable way for you to gain insights into not only how to delegate better next time but also how to teach the team leaders in your unit or division to delegate to their own direct reports. Under pressure to produce, newly designated team leaders, or rookies, often "just do it" themselves because they fear losing control or overburdening others. But failure to delegate blocks their own staff members' advancement, making those employees resentful and then disengaged.

Here are several ideas that can help you strengthen your team leaders' delegation skills:

- Explain that developing staff is as essential as attaining financial achievements.

- Lead by example. Trust and empower your rookie by delegating to him; you'll make it easier for him to engage his *own* team.

- Encourage the team leader to take small risks in playing to her staff's strengths. Early successes will build confidence.

- Help the person break complex projects into manageable chunks with clear milestones.

What You COULD Do.

Remember Martin's concern about how to support Joy in handling her delegated assignment?

Here's what the mentor suggests:

Joy doesn't have as much experience as Martin in dealing with problems in a product launch. Therefore, he should not assume that she can handle marketing deadlines. That would only be leaving her to flounder. It could jeopardize the launch as well as Joy's ability to prove herself and to take on more responsibility in the future. Delegating successfully is a matter of balancing support and unintrusiveness. Managers should provide only enough support to help the direct report succeed with the delegated task.

But support doesn't mean stepping in and mentioning his concerns directly to the marketing department. If Martin did that, he would be undermining the authority he has delegated to Joy. Although it is sometimes necessary for a manager to get directly involved after delegating a task, he should do so only when the direct report needs assistance or support. Preemptively stepping in to control a *potential* situation—even if doing so is convenient—does not demonstrate confidence in the direct report's ability to handle the situation.

Martin's challenge is to continue providing support without being intrusive. To strike the right balance, he should ask Joy how the planning is going and what she needs. He should point out the possible difficulties he sees ahead based on his experience with similar projects and the impact of marketing deadlines. And he should supply her with the information he learned about Marketing, because it may have a bearing on her assignment.

Tips and Tools

Tools for
Delegating Work

Delegation Skills Checklist

Use this checklist to learn how well you delegate. Answer all the following questions.

Question	Yes	No
1. Do you spend most of your time completing tasks that require your specific level of skill and authority?		
2. Do you assign tasks to people at the lowest staff level capable of completing them successfully?		
3. Do you have trust and confidence in the ability of your staff members to complete job assignments successfully?		
4. Do your staff members know what you expect of them?		
5. Do you take the time to carefully select the right person for the right job?		
6. Do you clearly brief staff members on all aspects of an assignment when you delegate?		
7. Do you allow employees sufficient time to solve their own problems before interceding with advice?		
8. Do you use delegation as a way to help employees develop new skills and provide challenging work assignments?		
9. Do you focus on results achieved versus the methods used to achieve them?		
10. Do you provide staff members with the necessary authority needed to complete assigned tasks?		
11. Do you realize that mistakes may be made and are an important part of the learning process for your staff?		
12. Do you clearly outline expected results and hold your staff accountable for achieving these results?		
13. Do you support your staff with an appropriate level of feedback and follow-up?		
14. Do you feel comfortable sharing control with your staff?		
15. Do you recognize that, as the delegator, you retain the ultimate responsibility for the outcome of the delegated assignment?		
TOTALS		

*If you answer **yes** to at least twelve questions, you are doing a good job of delegating.*

*If you answer **no** to three or more questions, you may want to enhance your delegation skills. For the **no** questions, you may want to identify how to change the behavior and practice it the next time you delegate an assignment.*

Worksheet for Preparing to Delegate

Use this worksheet to help you prepare for a delegating discussion with an employee.

Assignment:

Assigned to:

Clearly define the project, task, or function you are preparing to delegate.

What are the criteria for the assignment's success?

What is the timeline for completion?

Describe, in specific terms, the level of authority being delegated.

Describe your plan for follow-up to monitor progress.

Delegation Assignment Tracking Form

Use this form to help you track the assignments you have delegated and monitor progress toward established goals.

Delegated tasks	Assigned to	Date assigned	Target due date	Date completed

Task Delegation Analysis

Once you have determined the tasks to delegate, use this form to help you plan each delegation and select the appropriate person for the job.

Task to delegate	Expected results	Established standards	Deadline	Skills needed	Possible personnel	Training needed

Test Yourself

This section offers ten multiple-choice questions to help you identify your baseline knowledge of delegation essentials. Answers to the questions are given at the end of the test.

1. When you're delegating, it is usually better to delegate responsibility for an entire task or project to one person rather than divide it among a number of people. True or false?

    a. True.

    b. False.

2. How can delegating increase overall productivity and efficiency?

    a. By matching skills with people, you make the best use of organizational resources.

    b. By reducing your level of stress, you become more productive.

    c. By focusing on team efforts rather than individual efforts, you build morale.

3. What approaches might you consider using to determine what and how to delegate?

    a. By seniority, job responsibility, or team.

    b. By task, project, or function.

    c. By who volunteers within a team or among your direct reports.

4. Occasionally, you may need to consider bringing in resources from outside your organization. In addition to checking references and getting written proposals, what should you examine?

  a. The additional time needed to manage outside consultants or temporary workers.

  b. Additional long-term costs of outside resources.

  c. How it might look to your supervisor if you don't do the work yourself.

5. Which of the following actions is *not* an example of delegating by project?

  a. Conducting a customer survey.

  b. Writing a memo requesting feedback on a recent group presentation.

  c. Training the team on a new computer system.

6. What set of questions might you want to *first* ask yourself about a task that could help you delegate it appropriately to the right person?

  a. What thinking skills are needed for this task? What activities must be performed? What interpersonal skills are needed to complete the task?

  b. Who has the time available to complete this task? Who has done this kind of task before? Who has the right equipment available?

c. When does the task need to be completed? Who will do it the way you want it to be done? Who will not resent having the additional work?

7. Is it OK to use delegation as a way of testing an employee's capabilities before proceeding with a promotion?

a. Yes. It's a way to check the match between the employee's skills and the requirements of the new position.

b. No. It's not fair to ask an employee to demonstrate a different set of capabilities from those required for his or her current position.

8. Which of the following best describes reverse delegation?

a. You take back an assignment you delegated to someone else in order to complete it effectively.

b. Someone to whom you delegated an assignment wants to return it to you or expects you to solve problems or make decisions related to the assignment.

9. When might it be best to take back a delegated assignment from an employee?

a. When completing the task yourself would take less time than offering support to the employee.

b. When completion of the task appears to be out of control, and your management capability may be on the line.

c. When critical deadlines might be missed without assistance from you or others.

10. Does it make more sense to delegate to the most experienced individual available, or to the person with the lowest possible skill level required to perform the task effectively?

   a. Delegate to the most experienced individual available.

   b. Delegate to the person with the lowest possible skill level required to perform the task.

Answers to test questions

1, a. It's true: delegating an entire task or project to one person helps eliminate confusion and encourages initiative and problem solving. If that person then involves others, it is still clear who is ultimately responsible for the outcome.

2, a. Delegating effectively can increase overall productivity by making the best use of organizational resources. In addition, delegating can increase the time available to you for focusing on higher-level tasks such as long-term planning, policy development, and projects that require your skills and authority.

3, b. Delegating by task involves assigning specific tasks or subtasks to individuals. Delegating by project involves a group of tasks related to a specific objective. Delegating by function involves groups of tasks related to a type of activity, such as marketing, sales, or training.

4, a. You will need to find time to manage any outside consultants or temporary workers. On the positive side, however, outside resources can fill short-term gaps in staffing and may save time and money over the long term.

5, b. Writing a memo requesting feedback on a presentation is a *task* delegation and not a *project* delegation.

6, a. Before you delegate, consider the skills needed, the physical activities involved, and whether or not strong interpersonal skills are required. Once you've identified the parameters of the task, you should compare the required skills with the availability, capabilities, and developmental needs of each of your staff members.

7, a. Using delegation to test an employee's capabilities can be helpful before you consider moving him into a new position. It gives both of you a chance to evaluate capabilities and to check the match of skills needed for the job. If the employee needs additional training, you can arrange for it as part of a developmental plan.

8, b. Reverse delegation occurs when the person to whom you have delegated a task wants to give it back or expects you to fix problems related to it. Although you may want to step in and help, resist the urge. This situation gives you an opportunity to build trust and confidence by helping the individual complete the task. For this reason, you should try to avoid taking back a delegated task.

9, c. If major problems surface—such as missing a critical deadline—that will seriously undermine other projects, you may need to take back a delegated assignment. However, try to support the employee in completing the assignment in any way possible. For example, consider taking back only part of the assignment or offering additional resources.

10, b. To make the best use of staff resources, always delegate to the person at the lowest possible skill level required. Frequently, delegating to the lowest needed skill level also builds employees' capabilities more quickly, making more experienced employees available for new challenges.

Frequently Asked Questions

How can I avoid having my staff members feel that I'm dumping work on them?

- Balance the assignment of tasks seen as tedious or difficult with tasks and projects that spark staff interest, can be enjoyable, and may gain them recognition by others.

- To promote a sense of shared responsibility for jobs seen as boring or unpleasant, split these tasks or projects among more than one staff member as well as yourself.

- Seek input from your staff about the types of assignments they find interesting and challenging.

- Clearly communicate the benefits and opportunities from their point of view.

Is it OK to use delegation as a way of testing a staff member's capabilities before proceeding with a promotion?

Yes! It can actually be helpful to a staff member to have an opportunity to assume some of the responsibilities related to a new position. It gives both of you a chance to evaluate capabilities and check the match of skills needed for the job. If additional training is required, it can be implemented as part of a development plan or the promotion.

What if I can't find a staff member with the skills I need to complete a task?

- Train or coach someone to develop the skills you need.

- Consider looking outside your group or your organization for the expertise you need. You may be able to borrow a staff member who would like the opportunity, or perhaps you can hire a temporary worker for a short or fixed duration.

- Review the task to see whether you can divide it into subtasks for which one of your staff may have the needed skills.

How do I handle delegating upward?

- Delegating upward is a legitimate and appropriate request for assistance that requires escalation to a higher management level. It is not an attempt to dump a problem or issue back into a manager's hands.

- It is important for managers to understand that they may need to advocate to senior management levels on behalf of a staff member responsible for a specific task or project.

To Learn More

Articles

Regina Fazio Maruca. "Fighting the Urge to Fight Fires: A Conversation with Carl Holmes." *Harvard Business Review* (November–December 1999).

> In this concise "Forethought" piece, Carl Holmes, formerly chief of the Oklahoma City Fire Department, discusses how hard it is to hand off responsibility to others when you've worked your way through the ranks. There's always the temptation to perform the very tasks you're supposed to be overseeing. But delegating responsibility is a critical part of being a good leader. Nowhere is that fact more apparent than in the field of firefighting, where efficient leadership can literally mean the difference between life and death. Holmes describes the radical steps he took to get his battalion chiefs to stop fighting fires and instead to start doing their real jobs—managing their people. His insights offer valuable lessons for any new manager seeking to master delegation.

William Oncken Jr. and Donald L. Wass. "Management Time: Who's Got the Monkey?" *Harvard Business Review* (November 1999).

> In this classic article, the authors show what can happen when reverse delegation is allowed to run amok. Managers who can't

resist stepping in to solve employees' problems or take back a delegated task end up having no time to carry out their real responsibilities. Oncken and Wass (as well as Steven Covey in an afterword to the article) offer numerous suggestions for cultivating a sense of initiative in your employees so that they develop the skills and confidence required to handle their own problems rather than transfer them to your shoulders.

David Stauffer. "The New Thinking on High-Control Management: Set Boundaries Instead." *Harvard Management Update* (November 1997).

Effective managers are always challenged by the question of how much they should control and how much they should let go. This article proposes that managers relinquish some control and instead set boundaries within which employees are free to accomplish their work within "a rather large solution space." The article describes the time and place to set boundaries, the importance of selecting which managerial responsibilities to retain and which to delegate, and the need to overcome false assumptions about your employees.

Books

Linda A. Hill. *Becoming a Manager: How New Managers Master the Art of Leadership*. Harvard Business School Press, 2003.

In this book, Hill examines the wide range of challenges people face when they move from an individual contributor or entrepreneur role to a managerial role for the first time. For many novice managers, learning to delegate and develop people rather than carry out tasks themselves is a difficult challenge. Hill shares excerpts from interviews she conducted with new managers and provides her own insights based on years of research. She thus puts a human face on the issue, showing readers that they're not alone and helping them see that delegating can be mastered.

Kate Keenan. *The Management Guide to Delegating*. Horsham, West Sussex: Ravette Publishing, 1996.

In this short and informative book, Keenan provides a comprehensive overview of the key elements of delegation. Topics include the following: determining why and what to delegate, deciding who can do it, briefing and monitoring, and understanding attitudes about delegating. Each chapter concludes with a list of questions to ask oneself as well as tips for improving delegation skills.

Bob Nelson, Burton Morris, and Ken Blanchard. *1001 Ways to Energize Employees*. New York: Workman Publishing Company, 1997.

This practical handbook, which includes case studies, examples, techniques, and research highlights, is filled with suggestions for increasing employee involvement and enthusiasm.

Andrew E. Schwartz. *Delegating Authority*. New York: Barron's Business Success Series, 1992.

This handy pocket guide to delegation gives new as well as experienced managers an overview of the essential skills and techniques for delegating effectively. It discusses delegation in terms of five key components: goal setting, communication, motivation, supervision, and evaluation. There are recommendations for specific techniques and approaches within each component.

Stephanie Winston. *The Organized Executive: A Program for Productivity*. New York: Warner Books, 1994.

This book addresses the specifics of controlling paperwork, filing systems, and computer systems, and managing a schedule for efficiency. Each chapter addresses a specific organizational issue and provides concise how-to steps. The book has checklists and worksheets to work through the strategies listed.

Other Learning Sources

Harvard Business School Publishing. *Case in Point*. Boston: Harvard Business School Publishing, 2004.

Case in Point is a flexible set of online cases designed to help prepare middle- and senior-level managers for a variety of leadership challenges. These short, reality-based scenarios provide sophisticated content that offer a focused view of the realities of the life of a leader. Topics include aligning strategy, removing implementation barriers, overseeing change, anticipating risk, and making ethical decisions. You'll also read about building a business case, cultivating customer loyalty, understanding emotional intelligence, and developing a global perspective. Other topics include fostering innovation, defining problems, selecting solutions, managing difficult interactions, understanding the coach's role, delegating for growth, managing creativity, influencing others, managing performance, providing feedback, and retaining talent.

Harvard Business School Publishing. *Influencing and Motivating Others*. Boston: Harvard Business School Publishing, 2001.

Have you ever noticed that some people seem to have a natural ability to stir people to action? *Influencing and Motivating Others* provides actionable lessons on getting better results from direct reports (influencing performance), greater cooperation from your peers (lateral leadership), and stronger support from your own boss and senior management (persuasion). Managers will learn the secrets of lateral leadership (leading peers), negotiation and persuasion skills, and ways to distinguish between effective and ineffective motivation methods. Through interactive cases, expert guidance, and activities for immediate application at work, this program helps managers assess their ability to effectively persuade others, measure motivation skills, and enhance employee performance.

Harvard Business School Publishing. *Managing Direct Reports*. Boston: Harvard Business School Publishing, 2000.

Learn the skills and concepts you need for effectively managing direct reports, and apply these techniques immediately to your own situation. Through interactive practice scenarios, expert guidance, on-the-job activities, and a mentoring fea-ture, you will learn and practice how to understand direct re-ports' expectations, manage a network of relationships, and delegate along a continuum. Pre- and post-assessments and additional resources complete the workshop, preparing you for more productive direct report relationships.

Sources for Delegating Work

We would like to acknowledge the sources we used in developing this topic.

Timothy W. Firnstahl, "Letting Go," *Harvard Business Review* (September–October 1986).

Lauren Keller Johnson, "Are You Delegating So It Sticks?" *Harvard Management Update* (July 2004).

Kate Keenan, *The Management Guide to Delegating* (Horsham, West Sussex: Ravette Publishing, 1996).

Robert B. Maddux, *Delegating for Results* (Menlo Park, CA: Crisp Publishers, 1990).

William Oncken Jr. and Donald L. Wass, "Management Time: Who's Got the Monkey?" *Harvard Business Review* (November 1, 1999).

Carol A. Walker, "Save Your Rookie Managers from Themselves," *Harvard Business Review* (April 2002).

Susan Wilson, *Goal Setting* (New York: AMACOM, 1994).

Stephanie Winston, *The Organized Executive: A Program for Productivity* (New York: Warner Books, 1994).

Notes

Notes

Notes

Notes

Notes

Notes

Notes

How to Order

Harvard Business Press publications are available worldwide from your local bookseller or online retailer.

You can also call:
1-800-668-6780

Our product consultants are available to help you 8:00 a.m.–6:00 p.m., Monday–Friday, Eastern Time. Outside the U.S. and Canada, call: 617-783-7450.

Please call about special discounts for quantities greater than ten.

You can order online at:
www.HBSPress.org